Four Square (4) Writing Method

for Grades 1-3

Written by Judith S. Gould and Evan Jay Gould

Illustrated by Mary Galan Rojas

Teaching & Learning Company

1204 Buchanan St., P.O. Box 10
Carthage, IL 62321-0010

This book belongs to

_____

Acknowledgments

Thanks to the students, administration and staff of Windy Hill Elementary School and R.M. Paterson Elementary School for piloting the program and believing in it.

Thanks to Mary Burke for starting the "squaring" and having the chutzpa to make us do this.

Thanks to Peter Correa and Barbara Najdzion for technical and artistic support.

Cover photos by Images and More Photography

Pictures © Corel Corporation

Copyright © 1999, Teaching & Learning Company

ISBN No. 1-57310-188-5

Printing No. 16 15

Teaching & Learning Company
1204 Buchanan St., P.O. Box 10
Carthage, IL 62321-0010

Table of Contents

Dear Teacher or Parent,

In collegiate studies of elementary education, future teachers learn about the importance of writing as a language art. Elementary education students are told that it is a vital form of expression and a communication skill which is required for the work force of the future. Writing is touted as being an interdisciplinary link for classroom teachers to apply almost universally. Today's teachers are aware of the authentic assessments that students will face and that the basic language arts skills are vital to their success.

Even while writing has taken a stronger role in the schools, a gap has developed at the primary and secondary levels. High school teachers are quick to point out that students arrive without the skills to take an essay test or to write a term paper. Yet elementary education teachers have been reluctant to abandon current practices.

While this disparity has existed for a long time, it did not escalate to a crisis proportion until states began assessing the writing of their elementary age students. The disturbing results of the initial tests have proven that our children lack fundamental writing skills. Many cannot produce a focused, well-supported and organized composition.

Why don't we teach writing? When we teach children to read, we give them decoding skills to use. When we teach them science, we give them the scientific method. When we teach mathematics, we give them skills and drill specific facts and yet, we provide little skill instruction for writing but expect results.

In the following chapters we present a method of teaching basic writing skills that is applicable across grade levels and curriculum areas. It can be applied for the narrative, descriptive, expository and persuasive forms of writing. Prewriting and organizational skills will be taught through the use of a graphic organizer. This visual and kinesthetic aid is employed to focus writing, to provide detail and to enhance word choice. It is an excellent aid in preparing students for the demand/prompt draft writing assessments being given throughout the country.

Teaching writing through the use of a graphic organizer empowers students to write with confidence. Gloria Houston in her article "Learning How Writing Works" in the September 1997 issue of *Writing Teacher* states: "Visual organizers help students to conceptualize, understand, and structure a piece of written discourse successfully. Organizers eliminate 'jellyfish writing' and provide coherence and cohesiveness in a piece of writing."

We hope you can use the four square to help teach students writing, thought processes and study practices.

Sincerely,

Judith & Evan

Judith S. and Evan Jay Gould

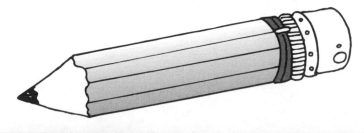

How to Use This Book

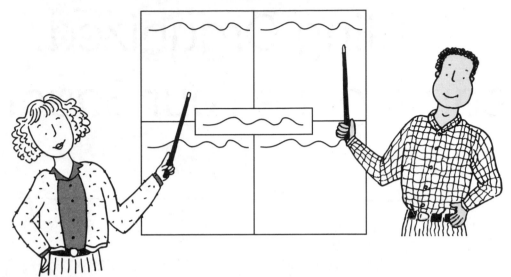

Four square instruction should be done at least biweekly-weekly in the primary grade classroom. It should be accompanied by other writing practice (e.g. shared writing, journals, letter writing, etc.).

Section 1
Getting Organized

This section focuses on the sequential instruction of the four square. It begins with activities that are appropriate for use with the youngest students. Steps one through five can be completed easily with students in the first grade. Steps six through 10 are designed for the second grade. Certainly, there will be the exceptional student, so feel free to take each child as far as he or she can go.

Section 2
Other Forms of Composition

Because our instruction is based on the expository style, we must make students aware of the other forms of writing and show them how to apply their skills. This section provides four square teaching tips and examples for the narrative, descriptive and persuasive styles.

Section 3
Samples of Four Square and Essays

This section provides completed organizers and corresponding essays for the four writing styles. These may be used as models for students or for your reference in instruction.

Section 4
Four Square and Beyond

Once the four square is learned, it is a handy tool for organizing thoughts across the curriculum. This section provides suggestions for use in the language arts program, the sciences, the arts and even mathematics. If the student is successful in four square writing, why not extend that success?

Section 5
Practice Prompts

This section contains reproducible practice pages that are appropriate for use once students have learned the organizer. There are examples in the expository and narrative styles.

Section 1
Getting Organized
Learning the Four Square

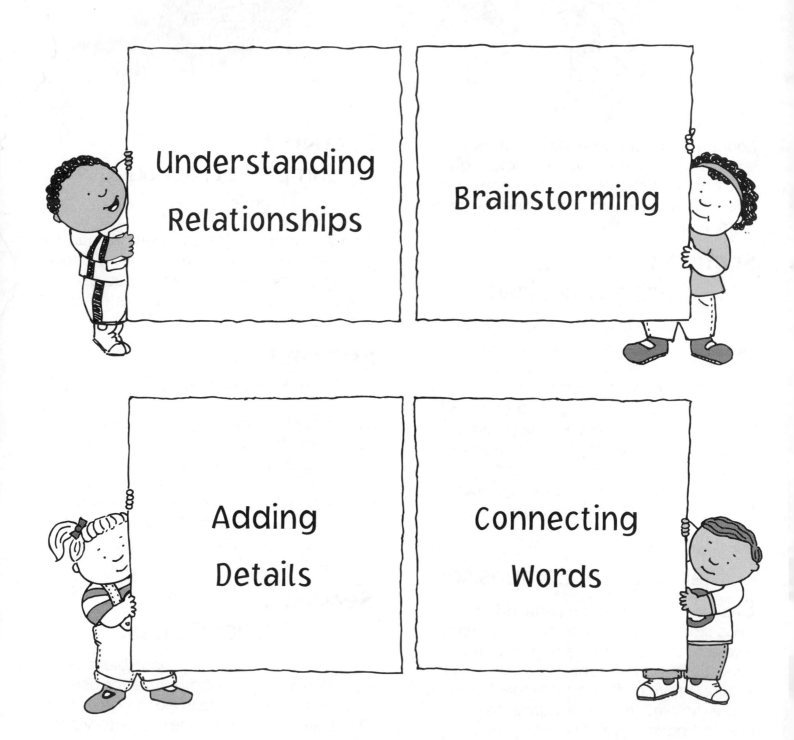

Understanding Relationships

Brainstorming

Adding Details

Connecting Words

Step 1

Categorizing
Understanding Similarities

Before writing takes place, a thought process must occur. If our desired outcome is a focused, organized and detailed composition, we must begin with even the youngest of our children to explore the relationships between ideas and objects. Reasoning is developed by classifying and categorizing the items in our everyday world. This reasoning can be developed into that prewriting thought process.

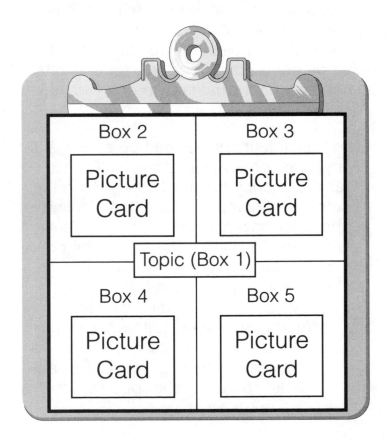

The initial activities in categorizing are best done using actual manipulative materials. A "brown bag" activity can be performed. In this activity the students are given bags full of random items. There may be toys, books, pencils, food or other common things. The students are then challenged to separate the items into different groups. Each group must have something that is the same about all items in the group. Sometimes a little modeling and coaching are necessary, but most children happily sort the items on the criteria of color, size or use.

The four square for use with picture card manipulation activities

After several repetitions with real items, this activity can then be done with picture cards. This moves the activity up one level of abstraction and towards producing written thought. At this stage the four square organizer can be introduced and used on a felt board or magnetic board with the appropriate backing on the picture cards.

We can introduce the four square early in the instruction of writing and prewriting to prepare students for its later use. Also, the four square will become a familiar and friendly format for organization and classification.

Once students have achieved mastery in the picture card exercise, they are ready for the more abstract cut-and-paste activity on the following pages. There is an additional level of abstraction involved, so it is important to allow students to develop the skills with the manipulative materials.

After practice with cut-and-paste activities, the students can be moved to a "blank four square" worksheet or journal page. The topic is written in the middle and the students must draw the items in the outer boxes. Encourage labeling of their pictures, and allow any spellings that they come up with at this point. It is recommended that the conventional spelling be penciled in because students often do not remember what they themselves have drawn or written.

The "blank four square" can be successfully used as a daily journal page. The students can copy the word that goes in the center and complete the categorization in the outer boxes. Topics for this activity are nearly limitless. Pages can be done as you study shapes, numbers and colors. Four squares can be completed on a letter being studied by simply drawing four items that begin with the letter sound. Common items can be classified by writing toys, foods, animals, sports or other popular topics in the center.

These activities are fun and non-threatening and should be within the ability of children with the least amount of early childhood literacy training.

Name _____

Directions: Cut out pictures that belong in the four square and paste in the four boxes.

Pets

Name _____

Directions: Cut out pictures that belong in the four square and paste in the four boxes.

Food

Name _____

Directions: Cut out pictures that belong in the four square and paste in the four boxes.

Toys

Name _____

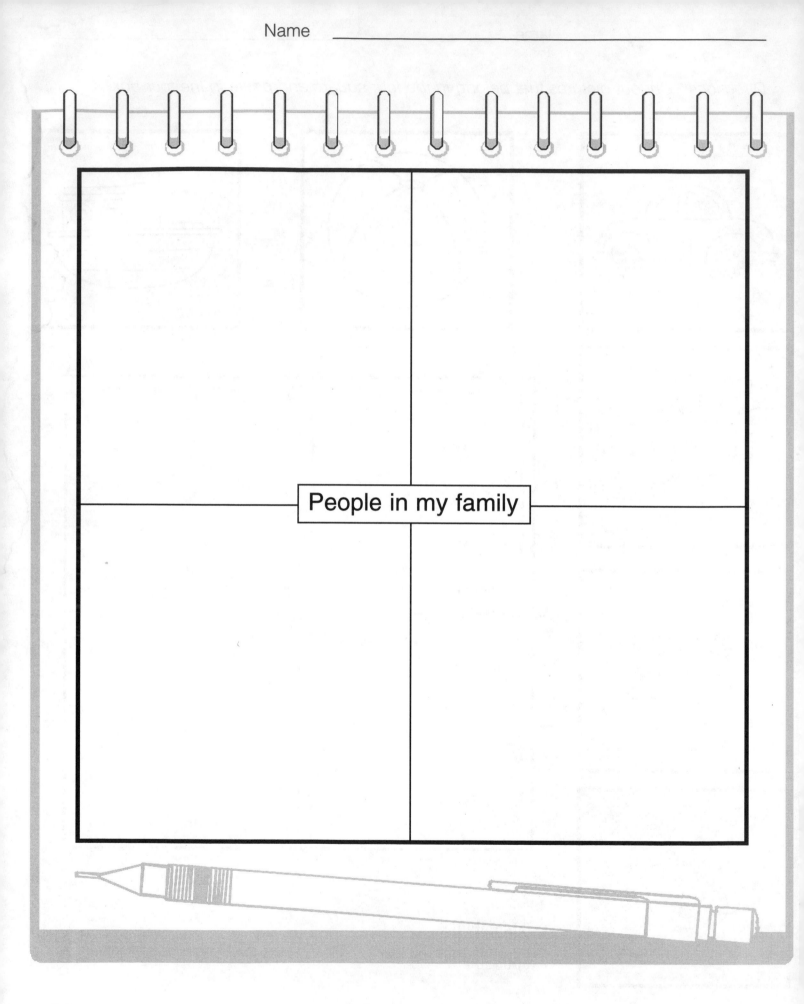

People in my family

Snacks I like to eat

ink

Name _____

Step 2

Labeling Writing with a Summary Sentence

Using a "Feeling" Sentence to Complete a Four Square

By now students have gained a level of comfort using the four square as a format for compiling like ideas. Most children should be writing the word to represent their illustrations, or at least writing the beginning and final consonants with coaching.

The next activity asks students to write a single sentence to summarize their feelings about a topic. They will now need to give only three examples of the topic. They will use the sentence to complete their four square, and it will later be developed to the final sentence of a paragraph.

To write this sentence students should be prompted to think about the topic and how it makes them feel. The sentence should have the topic and an emotion word in it. If needed, a cloze activity (____ makes me feel ____) can be used. Ample modeling and practice ensure success with this sentence writing activity. You may choose to use a word bank to facilitate the spelling at this level.

a four square
with a concluding
feeling sentence

Directions: Give three examples and a feeling sentence.

_____

_____

Games

_____

Feeling Sentence: _____

_____

_____

_____

_____

_____

Directions: Give three examples and a feeling sentence.

_____

_____

Zoo Animals

_____

Feeling Sentence: _____

_____

_____

_____

_____

_____

Name _____

_____

_____

Insects

Feeling Sentence: _____

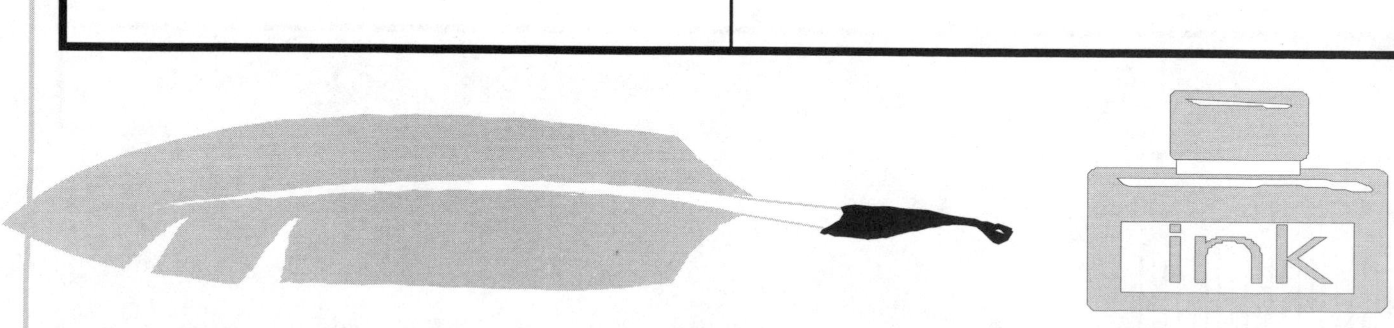

_____

_____

_____

_____

_____

_____

ink

Name ______________________________

Directions: *Give three examples and a feeling sentence.*

Vegetables

____

____

____

Feeling Sentence: ____________

____

____

____

____

____

____

Step 3

Placing a Sentence in the Center of the Four Square

Using Reasons Instead of Examples

Now the stage has been set for some reasoning and persuasion. The next step involves only a small change in the challenge. The center box will now contain a complete sentence. In previous exercises there was only one word or short phrase. The introduction of a complete sentence now alters the requirements for the outer boxes. These boxes must now contain full sentences which state **reasons, examples or explanations** that prove the center box true. These reasons, examples or explanations must all be different from one another and must be real, quantifiable reasons, not merely matters of opinion.

Being somewhat egocentric, children may not easily identify the distinction between fact and opinion. If they believe that "fun," "cool" and "awesome" are quantifiable and different from one another, they will have difficulty building a good persuasive or expository piece. To help kids understand that perceptions are very different and that an opinion is not reliable, start by telling them two stories.

Story 1

Teacher: I have just heard a great song. It is cool, awesome and great. Do you want to hear it?

Students: (shouting) Yeah!

Teacher: Great. I didn't know you were into opera!

Point out that opera is cool, awesome and great to you, but you may not wish to endure any music that is cool, awesome and great to them.

Story 2

Teacher: I've got a great new food here. It's delicious, wonderful and so tasty.

Students: (if they fall for it a second time) Yeah!

Teacher: Great. I didn't know you kids liked liver.

For further practice in developing strong or persuasive reasons and examples, encourage students to "prove" the prompting sentence. Even at this stage the children can be prepared for persuasive and expository writing.

A "Prove It!" reproducible worksheet is provided on page 22 for extra practice on this skill.

The four square with a complete sentence in the center. Boxes 2, 3 and 4 now contain sentences which prove the topic. Box 5 remains a "feeling" sentence.

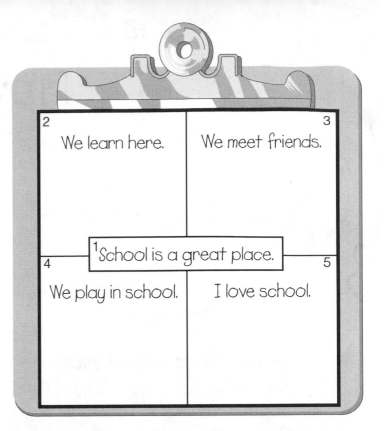

Students should still be encouraged to illustrate these four squares. The use of a word bank or a word wall may facilitate spelling. It is recommended that a four square be completed in draft using "temporary" spelling and then corrected to publish with conventional spelling.

Be sure to read the four square aloud as a "story" upon completion; this will facilitate the transfer to paragraph writing. Our story would read:

School is a great place. We learn here. We meet friends. We play in school. I love school.

The four square at this stage can easily be turned into a mini book by cutting the boxes apart. A front and back cover can be added to make a published work. Writing a picture book of his or her own is a wonderful boost to the young child's budding sense of accomplishment.

Reproducible workbook pages and "book making" blanks follow.

Prove It!

Directions: Choose the answer or answers that best prove the statement true.

1. My school is the best in the world.
   a. It's cool
   b. They pay us to attend
   c. I like it
   d. Candy in the lunchroom

2. The beach makes a good vacation.
   a. Awesome
   b. Super
   c. Cool water
   d. Soft sand

3. Pizza is the best food.
   a. It rules
   b. It's inexpensive
   c. It tastes the best
   d. It has all food groups

4. Basketball is a great sport.
   a. Exciting to watch
   b. Fun to play
   c. Mega, mega cool
   d. It's groovy

5. Dr. Seuss is a wonderful author.
   a. He's the best
   b. He's great
   c. The stories rhyme
   d. The pictures are colorful

"Prove It!" exercise may be completed orally or reproduced to transparency.

Name _____

Directions: Write three sentences that prove the topic. Then write a feeling sentence.
You may draw pictures to go with your sentences.

_____

_____

_____

_____

_____

_____

Summer is a great season.

_____

_____

_____

Feeling Sentence: _____

_____

_____

_____

_____

_____

Name _____

Directions: Write three sentences that prove the topic. Then write a feeling sentence. You may draw pictures to go with your sentences.

I like to visit the zoo.

Feeling Sentence: _____

24

Name _____

Directions: Write three sentences that prove the topic. Then write a feeling sentence. You may draw pictures to go with your sentences.

_____
_____
_____

_____
_____
_____

Field trips are great.

_____
_____
_____

Feeling Sentence: _____

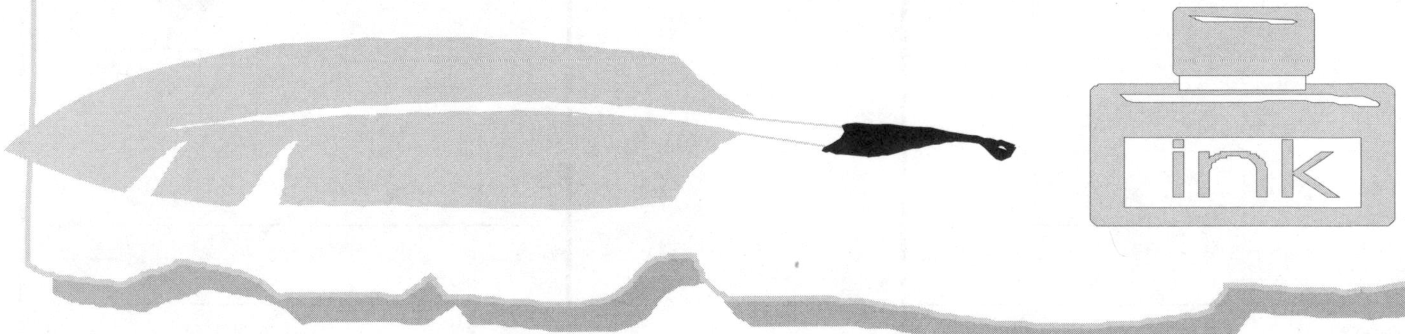

_____

_____

_____

_____

_____

_____

ink

Mini Four Square Books

Directions: Complete the four square and illustrate. Then cut along lines. You may make construction paper covers. Staple together to form a "book."

My family is special.

Mini Four Square Books

Directions: Complete the four square and illustrate. Then cut along lines. You may make construction paper covers. Staple together to form a "book."

My class is great.

Mini Four Square Books

Directions: Complete the four square and illustrate. Then cut along lines. You may make construction paper covers. Staple together to form a "book."

I like to have friends.

Step 4

Writing a Paragraph

Taking It Off of the Organizer

When considering that a paragraph is simply a bunch of sentences on the same topic, it becomes clear that even these young writers are ready to tackle the feat of writing a paragraph. In actuality, students have been writing paragraphs, only in the shape of a four square, rather than a conventional paragraph style.

Because the completed four squares have been read orally in the previous steps of instruction, students are familiar with the order of composition and the movement through the four square. They will now simply transfer those skills from the four square and onto lined writing paper for paragraph building. For the instruction of the paragraph form, it is best to use a whole class model. A four square can be built in the large group, using a sentence in each outer box, and a feeling sentence in the last box. It is then read aloud in the usual fashion.

Two Rules for Paragraphs

1. Indent the first word only.
(Two fingers placed on the paper's edge or margin)

2. Fill the line completely.
(No blank spaces at the end of a line. Each sentence need not start on its own line.)

The two rules for paragraph writing are then introduced. It is valuable to display a "chapter book" to students; it lets them know that paragraph writing is really for the "big kids."

The teaching of the form should be done in a rote fashion, where each sentence is modeled on chart paper or a chalkboard, then copied by individual students. Be sure to circulate as each sentence is written to be sure that students have grasped the basic technical skills to manipulate the text.

Directions:
Complete the four square with three sentences and a feeling sentence. Then write the paragraph on the lines below.

It is great to have a pet.

Feeling Sentence: _____

_____

_____

_____

_____

_____

30

Directions:
Complete the four
square with three
sentences and a
feeling sentence.
Then write the
paragraph on the
lines below.

_____   _____

_____   _____

_____   _____

_____   _____

| The playground is fun. |

_____   Feeling Sentence: _____

_____   _____

_____   _____

_____   _____

_____

_____

_____

_____

_____

_____

Name _____

Directions:
Complete the four square with three sentences and a feeling sentence. Then write the paragraph on the lines below.

_____ _____ _____ _____ _____	_____ _____ _____ _____

Music class is great.

_____ _____ _____ _____	Feeling Sentence: _____ _____ _____ _____

_____

_____

_____

_____

_____

_____

32

Step 5

4□ + 1

Adding More Details

Once a level of mastery is achieved with the five-sentence paragraph, students can begin to build an eight-sentence paragraph. The writing needs to be moved back into the four square in order to maintain focus and purpose in the writing. By adding one additional detail sentence in each box, the students are elaborating on the original reason, example or explanation. Elaboration of a point is requisite of good writing, and even first graders are able to accomplish this using the four square plus one formula.

To elicit the student responses in adding the "plus one" details, it may be useful to ask for an example; tell more about it or tell us what is so great about it. At this level students are asked to keep using full sentences in their four square writing. Mastery of this level is typically achieved by the end of the first grade year.

It is advisable to teach, reinforce and practice the addition of detail while in the four square format. The movement to paragraph form on lined writing paper will be more successful if there is a good understanding of the relationship of ideas. For instance, in the "learning" box of our four square plus one (on the next page) we needed to add a detail about learning. It would not have been appropriate to write a sentence about the cafeteria food! Modeling examples and non-examples of these details will help reinforce these ideas.

TLC10188 Copyright © Teaching & Learning Company, Carthage, IL 62321-0010

In addition to the individual and whole class practice, this activity can be used in a small group formation. Each group can draw a topic sentence from a bag or box. They are then given a four square form on an overhead transparency (reproducible to follow) and a wet-erase marker. The group can appoint a writer who will fill in the topic and write the suggestions of the other group members. Once completed, the group reporter can read the four square and present it to the whole class. They will enjoy seeing their work on the "big screen"!

On the following pages are reproducible worksheets for this step. These can be used for practice. Once students are able to build a four square plus one on their own, they may use their completed pages for practice in compiling this information into a paragraph.

Writing rich and detailed paragraphs at the primary level enables the students to engage in a "real" writing experience. A class chapter book can be written, and its authors will be a part of publishing and sharing a large piece of writing.

a four square plus one. It is recommended to use the same prompt repeatedly when introducing the steps because the familiarity will aid in instruction.

Our example would read:

School is a great place. We learn here. I like to learn science. We meet friends.

My best friend is in my class. We play in school. I like to play in centers. I love school.

We learn here.	We meet friends.
I like to learn science.	My best friend is in my class.
School is a great place.	
We play in school.	I love school.
I like to play in centers.	

34

Group: _____

Directions: Write a topic sentence and sentences that prove the topic. Then write a detail sentence in boxes 2, 3 and 4. Now write a feeling sentence. You may draw pictures to go with your sentences.

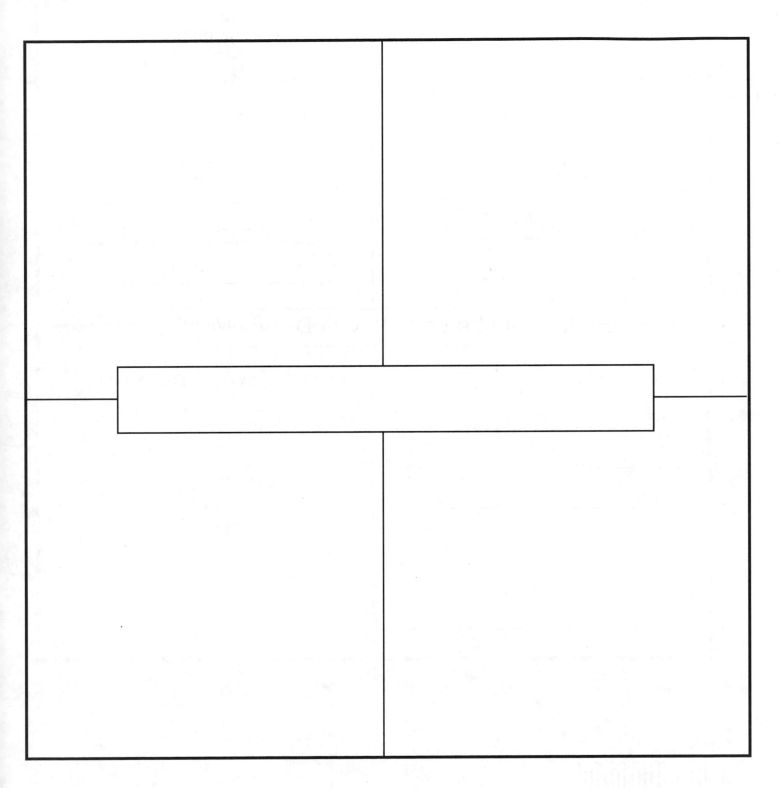

Name _____

Directions: Complete the four square plus one. Remember that the details should support the first sentence in the box.

It would be fun to meet Mickey.

Detail: _____

_____

_____

_____

_____

I would like to go on the rides.

Detail: _____

_____

_____

_____

_____

It would be great to visit DisneyWorld.

The parade is great.

Detail: _____

_____

_____

_____

_____

I would love to go to DisneyWorld.

36

Name _____

Directions: Complete the four square plus one. Remember that the details should support the first sentence in the box.

The ice cream is so cool.

Detail: _____

_____

_____

_____

_____

The fudge is very chocolatey.

Detail: _____

_____

_____

_____

_____

I love hot fudge sundaes.

I like a cherry on top.

Detail: _____

_____

_____

_____

_____

Hot fudge sundaes make me feel happy.

ink

Directions: Complete the four square plus one. Remember that the details should support the first sentence in the box.

You can play with them.

Detail: _____

_____

_____

_____

_____

_____

They can keep you company.

Detail: _____

_____

_____

_____

_____

It is good to have a sister or brother.

They can help you.

Detail: _____

_____

_____

_____

_____

I love (would love) having a sister/brother.

Name _____

Directions: Complete the four square plus one. Remember that the details should support the first sentence in the box.

Reason: _____

_____

_____

Detail: _____

_____

_____

_____

Reason: _____

_____

_____

Detail: _____

_____

_____

_____

| My school is the best school. |

Reason: _____

_____

_____

Detail: _____

_____

_____

Feeling Sentence: _____

_____

_____

_____

_____

39

Step 6
Writing a Wrap-Up Sentence
The First Step in Preparing for the Multiple-Paragraph Essay

The activities included up to this step have been appropriate for the primary grades, where the reasonable goal is to write one well-supported paragraph with good detail and organization. However, the four square, by design, is a tool for writing a five-paragraph essay of the three-pronged-thesis-and-development type.

In order to move beyond the single paragraph, it is beneficial to put the writing back into the four square. In the earlier four square with a sentence for the topic, we developed three supporting sentences and a "feeling" sentence. In order to expand our writing, we will put aside this "feeling" sentence for the "wrap-up" sentence. We will also abbreviate the supporting ideas in the four square to a word or short phrase and eliminate the use of complete sentences. Four square will take on a role as more of a prewriting exercise, rather than a drafting tool.

We learn here.	We meet friends.
School is a great place.	
We play in school.	I love school.

4☐ with a feeling sentence

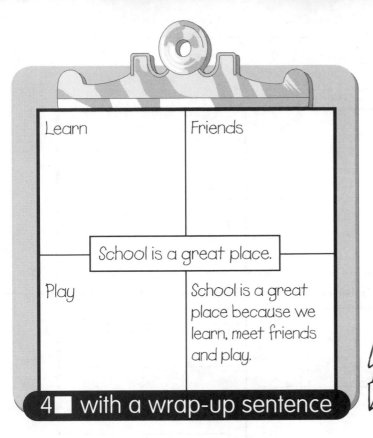

Learn	Friends
School is a great place.	
Play	School is a great place because we learn, meet friends and play.

4☐ with a wrap-up sentence

The "wrap-up" sentence is one sentence which includes both the topic and the supporting ideas together. It will later be developed into the introductory and concluding paragraphs.

Ah! Ah!
Ah! Ah!

One area of difficulty that you may encounter at this stage involves the introduction of a conjunction in the wrap-up sentence. *Since*, *Because* or *Due to* usually work nicely in this situation. At this stage of instruction we do not wish to get too caught up in technical matters, however, we can remind writers about the rules concerning a series sentence such as the wrap-up. With modeling and ample group practice (overhead transparency for sharing, too) students will quickly assimilate the language needed for a nicely flowing wrap-up sentence.

If a student is writing a wrap-up sentence without consideration of the flow of ideas, it can be read aloud in a straight monosyllabic monotone deemed the "Tarzan" voice. They will quickly come to understand that a sentence lacks flow when they hear it in this "jungle talk." They will seek to avoid a "Tarzan" sentence when they hear it read this way.

Name _____

Directions: Write a reason, example or explanation in each box to support the center box. Then write a wrap-up sentence to complete the four square.

It is important to have friends.

Wrap-Up Sentence:

_____

_____

_____

_____

My family is really special.

Wrap-Up Sentence:

_____

_____

_____

_____

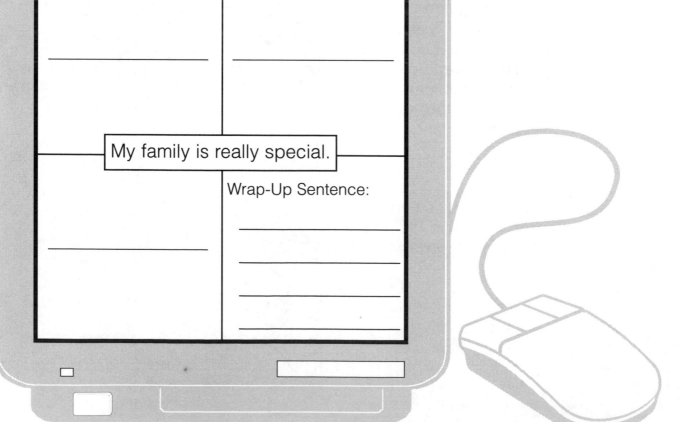

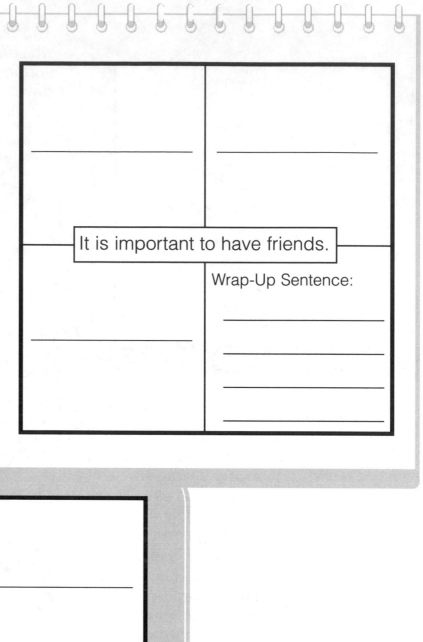

Name _____

Directions: Write a reason, example or explanation in each box to support the center box. Then write a wrap-up sentence to complete the four square.

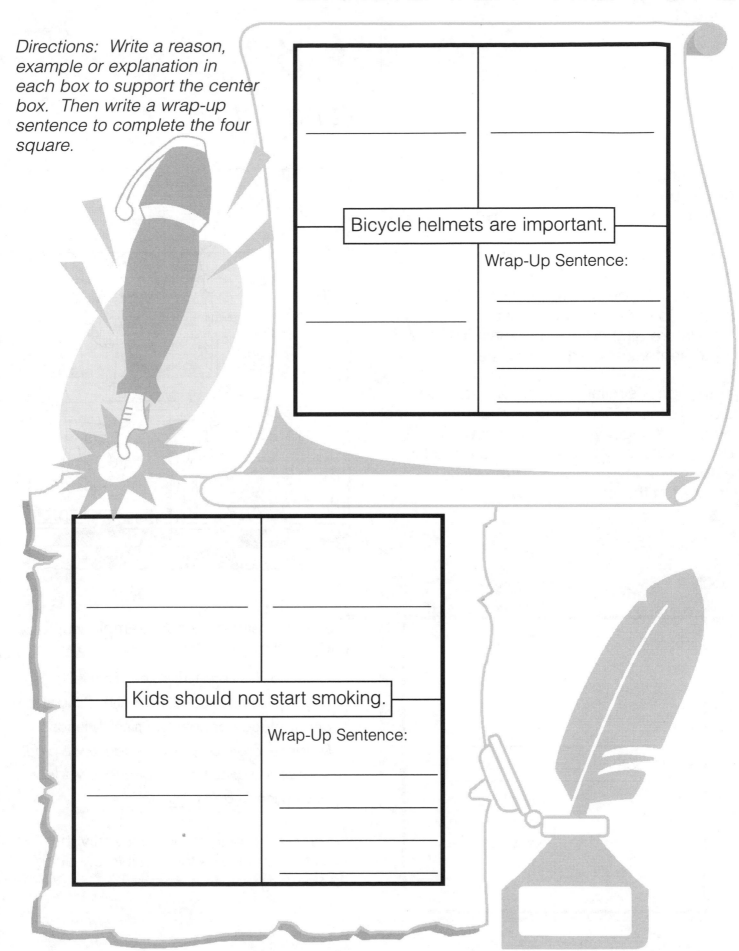

Bicycle helmets are important.

Wrap-Up Sentence:

_____
_____

_____
_____

Kids should not start smoking.

Wrap-Up Sentence:

_____
_____

_____

Step 7

4☐ + 3

adding Supporting Details

The reasons, examples or explanations developed in the previous step now need further development. In a sense, boxes 2, 3 and 4 will each be four squared independently. These details will make up the substance of the body paragraphs of our multiple-paragraph essay. Using the four square to develop these ideas ensures that details are aligned with the main ideas, and topic sentences start every paragraph.

Although a similar addition of detail took place in the 4 ☐ + 1 stage, students may not be so easily convinced of the need for detail. One way to point out the need for elaboration is to read aloud the story created in the previous step.

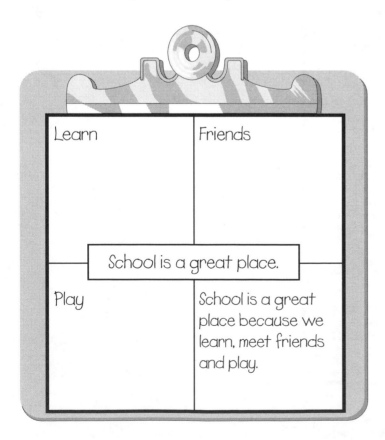

Learn	Friends
School is a great place.	
Play	School is a great place because we learn, meet friends and play.

The story created by our example would read as follows:

> School is a great place. School is a great place because we learn. School is a great place because we meet friends. School is a great place because we play. School is a great place because we learn, meet friends and play.

When read orally, students identify the repetition and need for detail to enhance the story.

44

Adding detail beyond the 4 □ + 1 step poses difficulty for some students. Many are not accustomed to elaborating. Writing is not like a multiple choice examination, and starting their brains may be painful for some kids!

Occasionally students will need some prompting to elaborate on their subject. For an item in box 2, 3 or 4, ask students to prove, clarify or give examples of the word phrase at the top of that box. Questions such as, "What's so good about this?" or "What is special about this reason/example?" often prompt the students to elaborate.

It is important to remind students that they may not repeat details from one box to another. Repetition equals boring composition!

although the writing is not being taken off the four square, it should be read aloud to show the formation of the essay.

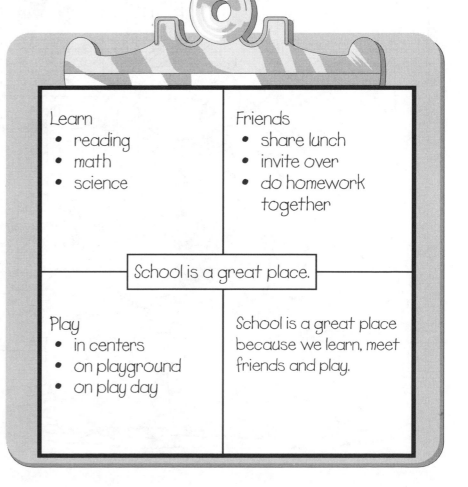

Our essay would read as follows:

School is a great place.

School is a great place because we learn. It is important to learn how to read. Math is an interesting subject to learn. When we learn science, we have lots of fun.

School is a great place because we meet friends. I like to share lunch with my friends. I can invite my friends over after school. My friends and I do our homework together.

School is a great place because we play. At center time everybody plays. We play on the playground during recess. Play day in the spring is a day when we just play and do no work at all.

School is a great place because we learn, make friends and play.

Because of the difficulty some students encounter during this step of instruction, it is recommended that there be ample opportunity for practice. Again, the lessons work well by following a sequence of modeling, group practice then individual assignments. The overhead transparency group project is terrific at this stage, and each group can have a recorder and a reporter who will read the story during sharing.

At this stage you can preview to students that they have "written" a five-paragraph essay!

46

Name _____

Directions: Write a reason, example or explanation in each box to support the main idea sentence in the center box. Then give three details for each. Write a wrap-up sentence.

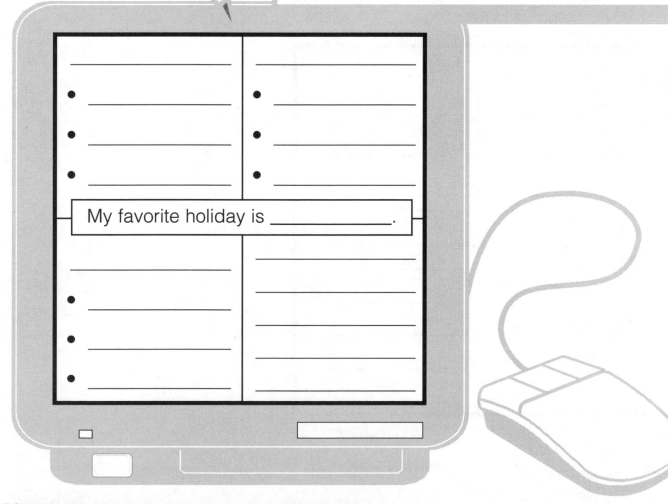

- _____
- _____
- _____

- _____
- _____
- _____

My school is the best.

- _____
- _____
- _____

- _____
- _____
- _____

My favorite holiday is _____.

Directions: Write a reason, example or explanation in each box to support the main idea sentence in the center box. Then give three details for each. Write a wrap-up sentence.

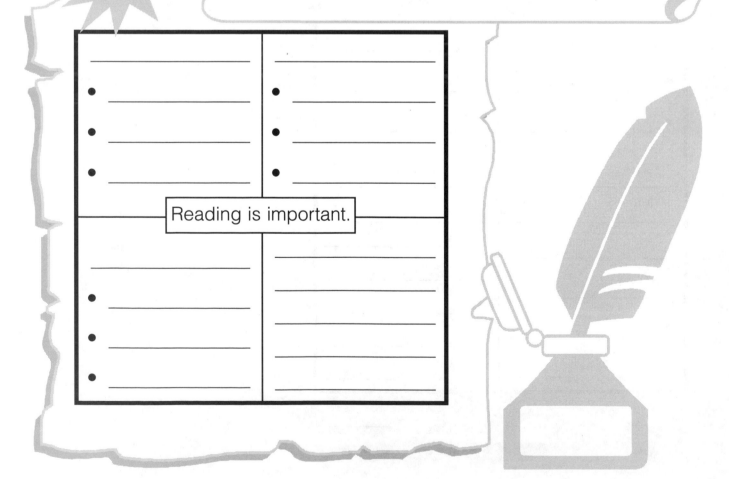

When I grow up I'd like to be a _____.

Reading is important.

Evaluating 4☐ + 3

A Checklist for the Teacher

When the students have achieved a general competency in the four square plus three stage, it is appropriate to give them a "writing test." Students (in this exam) should be given a one-sentence prompt for the center of their four square and given approximately 15 minutes to complete it. There is a need for expediting their thoughts because four square is a *prewriting* activity. Even when using an elaborate organizer, we still want kids spending most of their writing time on the composition itself.

Below is a checklist that is a useful instrument in evaluating four square plus three.

Evaluating 4☐ + 3

Student Name: _____

Topic: _____

		yes	no
1.	Are the four square reasons quantifiable and not opinions?	____	____
2.	Is there repetition of detail?	____	____
3.	Are the details logical expansion of the reasons?	____	____
4.	Are the details quantifiable and factual, free of opinion?	____	____
5.	Are there mechanical errors in the wrap-up sentence?	____	____

Step 8

$$4\square + 3 + C$$

Adding Connecting Words to Provide Transition Between Ideas

By now students are developing their thesis (box 1) into three reasons, examples or explanations (boxes 2, 3 and 4) and supporting elaboration. These ideas should be different from one another. These differences necessitate the use of transitions between ideas.

Transition words, or as the formula calls them CONNECTING words, can bridge the gap between ideas. If there are two similar ideas, there is an appropriate connecting word to link them. If ideas are contrasting, there are words that key us to the difference. These connecting words also provide smooth reading when changing paragraphs. Use of these words is critical to successful writing. In fact, it is so critical that students should not be asked to remember them. Color-code connecting words on wall posters and make available whenever they write (see pages 53-55).

To introduce the concept of connecting words to students, ask for a show of hands of those who have ever worked a puzzle. Most students can identify a puzzle piece and are familiar with its design. Explain that connecting words are the "little sticking out part" of the puzzle piece; they are words that do the same job as that part. Connecting words hold the different pieces of an essay together.

This explanation lends itself well to the presentation of the connecting word wall posters. To ensure success, the words are color coded. Because box 1 is the beginning of the piece, no color is necessary. Box 2 is coded green (*green* means "go"). Boxes 3 and 4 are yellow to signify moving along cautiously. Box 5 is red, for we are preparing to stop.

Students love choosing connecting words. They absolutely cannot get this step "wrong" so long as they select the word from the appropriate list. This fosters confidence in students, and this "easy" step is a break from the more intense brain work required in "+3."

Continue to read aloud all examples as they are completed. This will facilitate the change over to composition.

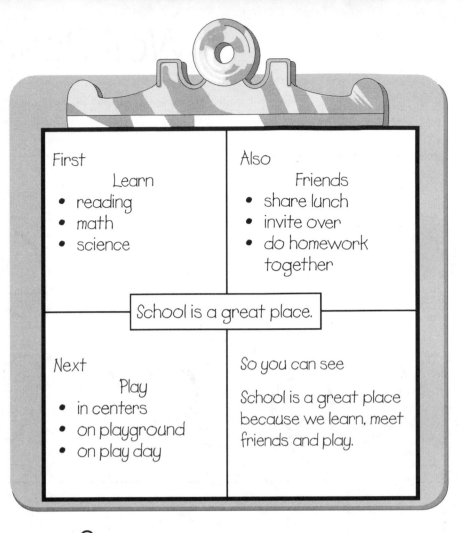

First
    Learn
- reading
- math
- science

Also
    Friends
- share lunch
- invite over
- do homework together

School is a great place.

Next
    Play
- in centers
- on playground
- on play day

So you can see

School is a great place because we learn, meet friends and play.

Our essay would read as follows:

School is a great place.

First, school is a great place because we learn. It is important to learn how to read. Math is an interesting subject to learn. When we learn science, we have lots of fun.

Also, school is a great place because we meet friends; I like to share lunch with my friends. I can invite my friends over after school. My friends and I do our homework together.

Next, school is a great place because we play. At center time everybody plays. We play on the playground during recess. Play day in the spring is a day when we just play and do not work at all.

So you can see, school is a great place because we learn, meet friends and play.

The following pages are wall posters and workbook pages for this step.

Wall Poster

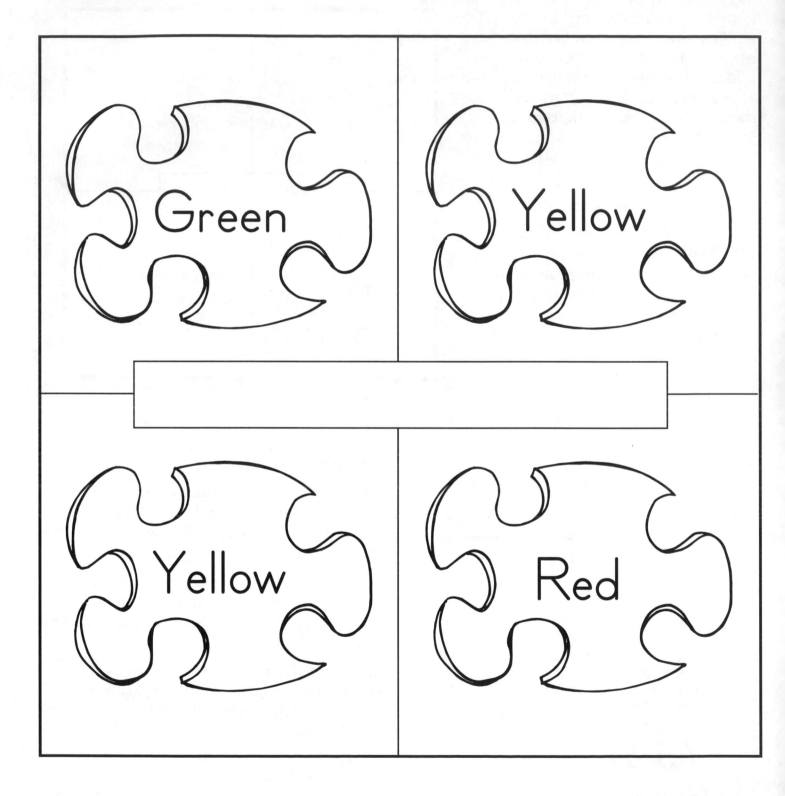

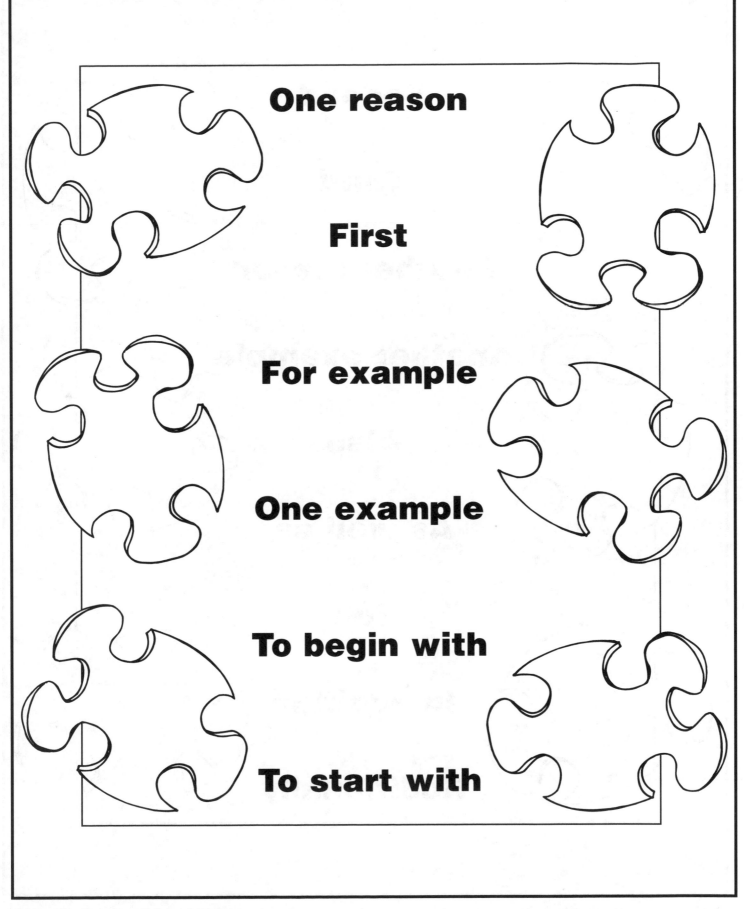

One reason

First

For example

One example

To begin with

To start with

Color the border of this poster green.

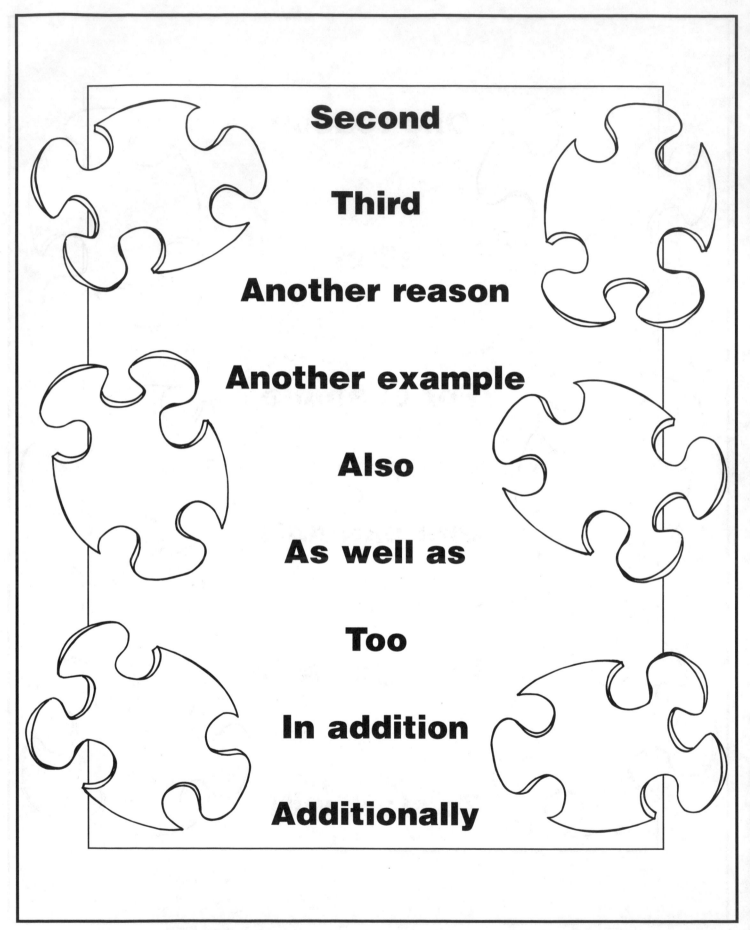

Second

Third

Another reason

Another example

Also

As well as

Too

In addition

Additionally

Color the border of this poster yellow.

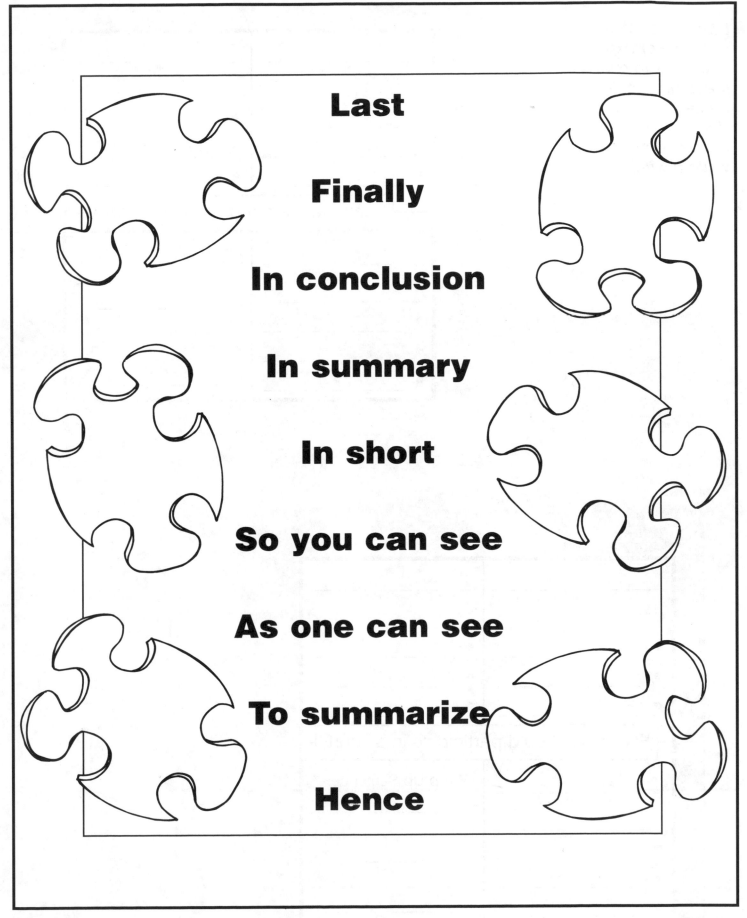

Last

Finally

In conclusion

In summary

In short

So you can see

As one can see

To summarize

Hence

Color the border of this poster red.

Name _____

Directions: Write a reason, example or explanation in each box to support the main idea sentence in the center box. Give three details for each. Then choose connecting words. Write a wrap-up sentence.

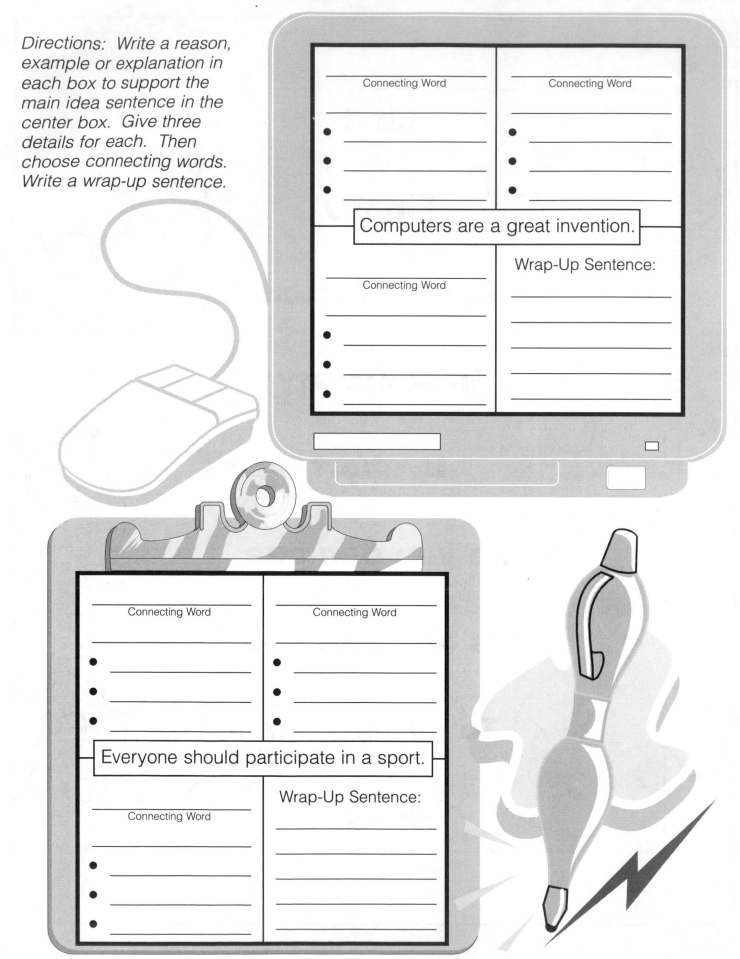

Connecting Word
_____
• _____
• _____
• _____

Connecting Word
_____
• _____
• _____
• _____

Computers are a great invention.

Connecting Word
_____
• _____
• _____
• _____

Wrap-Up Sentence:
_____
_____
_____
_____

Connecting Word
_____
• _____
• _____
• _____

Connecting Word
_____
• _____
• _____
• _____

Everyone should participate in a sport.

Connecting Word
_____
• _____
• _____
• _____

Wrap-Up Sentence:
_____
_____
_____
_____

56

Name _____

Directions: Write a reason, example or explanation in each box to support the main idea sentence in the center box. Give three details for each. Then choose connecting words. Write a wrap-up sentence.

Connecting Word

_____

- _____
- _____
- _____

Connecting Word

_____

- _____
- _____
- _____

My home state is the best in the U.S.

Connecting Word

_____

- _____
- _____
- _____

Wrap-Up Sentence:

_____
_____
_____
_____

Connecting Word

_____

- _____
- _____
- _____

Connecting Word

_____

- _____
- _____
- _____

Just say no to drugs.

Connecting Word

_____

- _____
- _____
- _____

Wrap-Up Sentence:

_____
_____
_____
_____

Rote Instruction
4□ + 3 + C = 5 Paragraphs
Taking the Writing Off the Organizer

Students have now spent a great deal of time working on the organizer, having never completed the composition phase of the writing process. The oral "story readings" performed with the completed four squares at early stages should have led to the understanding that this was a part of a bigger scheme.

When introducing the concept of moving the information from the four square to the multiple-paragraph essay, it is generally recommended to do a rote lesson. The whole class or group can build a four square together. Then the story is built, one sentence at a time. Use chart paper or an overhead transparency with a simulated piece of notebook paper.

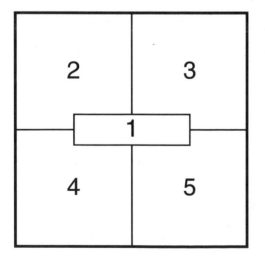

As the composition is being modeled one sentence at a time, students copy it. This "down time" can be used for instant remediation and reminders of the rules of writing in paragraphs. It would seem that no matter how many times a class is reminded to indent, students don't remember until they are reminded personally.

The four square has built in a good self-checking mechanism for sentence building. Since each of boxes 2, 3 and 4 have four items in them, students can be reminded to check for four capital letters and four periods in each of the corresponding paragraphs.

It is important to remind students never to take the shortcut of trying to list all items in each box as one, long sentence. Not only is this poor writing practice, but it is bound to be a run-on sentence.

On the following pages are exercises where the four square is given, and students need only make the transfer to the skill of composition.

Name _____

Directions: For the given four square, write the information in the five-paragraph format.

First	Also
Sleep Late	**Play Around**
• wear pajamas	• roller blade
• don't shower	• board games
• lie around	• cards

Weekends are great.

Next	In conclusion
Stay Up Late	Weekends are great because you can sleep late, play around and stay up late.
• sleepovers	
• scary movies	
• popcorn	

Paragraph 1

_____

_____

_____

_____

Paragraph 2

_____

_____

_____

_____

Paragraph 3

_____

_____

_____

_____

Paragraph 4

_____

_____

_____

_____

Paragraph 5

_____

_____

_____

_____

Did you indent each paragraph (five times)?
Do you have your capitals and periods?
Did you write from margin to margin?
Did you avoid Tarzan sentences?

Name _____

Directions: For the given four square, write the information in the five-paragraph format.

For example	Second
Honesty	**Pay Taxes**
• truthful always	• on time
• no cheating	• with pride
• admitting mistakes	• every year

A good citizen has many traits.

Too	Hence
Follow Laws	A good citizen has many traits such as honesty, paying taxes and following laws.
• traffic laws	
• don't steal	
• never fight	

Paragraph 1

_____

_____

_____

_____

_____

Paragraph 2

_____

_____

_____

_____

Paragraph 3

_____

_____

_____

_____

Paragraph 4

_____

_____

_____

_____

Paragraph 5

_____

_____

_____

_____

Did you indent each paragraph (five times)?
Do you have your capitals and periods?
Did you write from margin to margin?
Did you avoid Tarzan sentences?

Improving the Introductory Paragraph

Writing the "Thesis Statement"

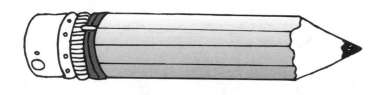

The introductory paragraph is perhaps the most important paragraph in a composition. It is the first impression made on the reader. Also, the first paragraph makes a promise. Explain to the students that the first paragraph in a composition sets the tone of the composition much in the way that a topic sentence sets the theme of the paragraph. The first paragraph will be used to promise the topic of discourse, as well as prepare the reader for the details to come.

First Paragraph

1. Topic Sentence
(Center of four square)

2. Wrap-Up Sentence
(Without connecting word)

3. Personal/Feeling Sentence

The beauty of the four square writing method is that nearly all the troubles faced in composition will be addressed in the organization stage of the writing process. Students at the primary level are rarely asked to write a thesis statement and paper, or at least they are not asked using that terminology. In the four square the students have prepared this information already. By writing the wrap-up sentence in box 5 very early in the learning of four square, students have already practiced this skill.

The first paragraph can now be expanded beyond the one-topic sentence. The topic sentence will start the composition. The wrap-up sentence will follow. For the third sentence, the students should write something reflective, thought provoking or a personal feeling. Using this formula gives readers comfort in reading an essay because they will know the topic, be prepared for coming reasoning and know the writer's feeling.

The final paragraph of our "school" essay:

School is a great place. It's great because we learn, meet friends and play at school. I wish I could go to school every day.

The following pages contain reproducible worksheet practice for building an introductory paragraph.

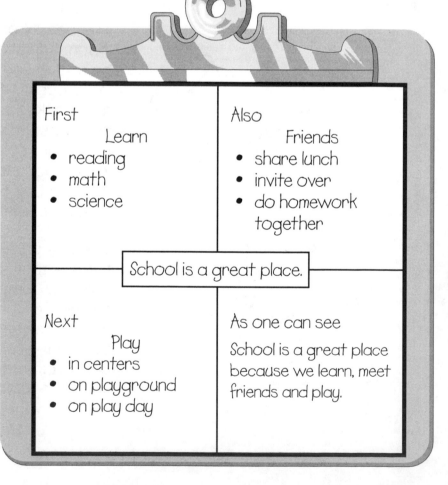

First
Learn
• reading
• math
• science

Also
Friends
• share lunch
• invite over
• do homework together

School is a great place.

Next
Play
• in centers
• on playground
• on play day

As one can see
School is a great place because we learn, meet friends and play.

64

Name _____

Directions: Write the first paragraph for each four square. Be sure to write the topic, the wrap-up and then a feeling sentence.

_____
_____
_____
_____
_____
_____
_____

Thanksgiving is my favorite holiday.

Thanksgiving is my favorite holiday because I see family, eat turkey and watch football.

It is important to get a good education.

It is important to get a good education so you can get a job, be successful and feel good about yourself.

_____
_____
_____
_____
_____
_____
_____

Name _____

Directions: Write the first paragraph for each four square. Be sure to write the topic, the wrap-up and then a feeling sentence.

_____
_____
_____
_____
_____
_____
_____

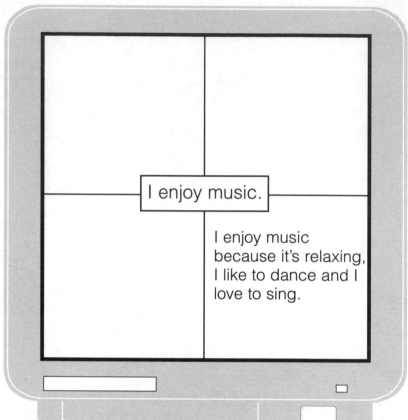

I enjoy music.

I enjoy music because it's relaxing, I like to dance and I love to sing.

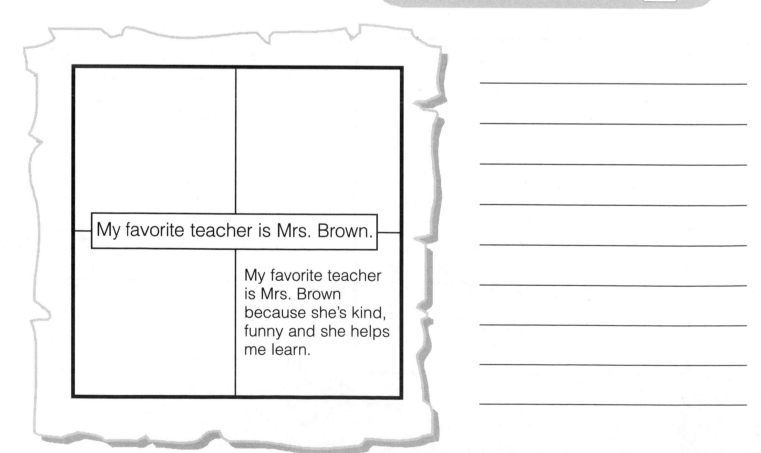

My favorite teacher is Mrs. Brown.

My favorite teacher is Mrs. Brown because she's kind, funny and she helps me learn.

_____
_____
_____
_____
_____
_____
_____
_____

Improving the Final Paragraph
Concluding the Composition

Second in importance only to the introductory paragraph, the concluding paragraph in composition carries a great deal of weight. In expository or persuasive writing, this is the writer's final chance to bring home the message to the reader. It is to be used for summary and final emphasis of the main idea.

Using the wrap-up sentence in combination with a "red" connecting word works well in bringing closure to the composition. The recounting of ideas should bring the reader full circle, and the connecting word signifies that this is the composition's end.

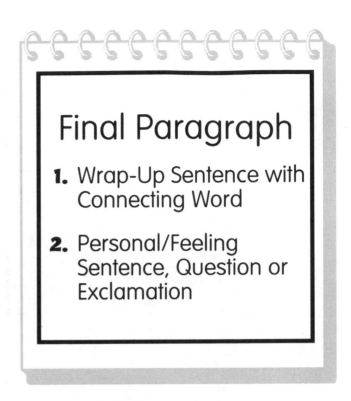

Final Paragraph

1. Wrap-Up Sentence with Connecting Word

2. Personal/Feeling Sentence, Question or Exclamation

This formula provides an easy way to conclude the composition. Encourage students to make that sentence perky!

At this point of the composition we do not want to add any new information, because it would not be developed. However, after the final wrap-up sentence it may be appropriate to add a reflective or personal sentence. Encouraging students to end with an exclamatory or declarative sentence usually gets them thinking. It is also an easy way to get them to add variety to sentence structure.

our "school" example

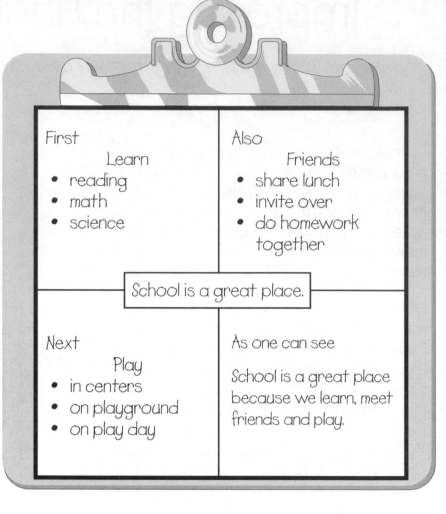

First
Learn
- reading
- math
- science

Also
Friends
- share lunch
- invite over
- do homework together

School is a great place.

Next
Play
- in centers
- on playground
- on play day

As one can see

School is a great place because we learn, meet friends and play.

The final paragraph of our "school" essay:

   As one can see, school is a great place because we learn, meet friends and play at school. I just love school, don't you?

The following pages contain reproducible worksheet practice for building a concluding paragraph.

68

Directions: Write the final paragraph for each four square. Be sure to write the wrap-up and a feeling sentence, question or exclamation.

_____

_____

_____

_____

_____

_____

_____

	My favorite dessert is pie a la mode.
	My favorite dessert is pie a la mode because I like the crust, the filling and the ice cream.

It is great to have a brother or sister.	
	It is great to have a brother or sister because he or she can keep you company, play with you and help you.

_____

_____

_____

_____

_____

_____

_____

Name _____

Directions: Write the final paragraph for each four square. Be sure to write the wrap-up and a feeling sentence, question or exclamation.

_____
_____
_____
_____
_____
_____
_____

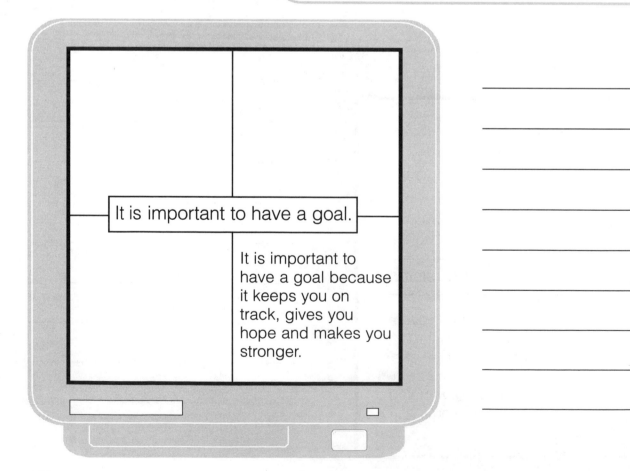

Everybody should recycle.

Everybody should recycle because we can save the Earth, help animals and have fewer garbage dumps.

It is important to have a goal.

It is important to have a goal because it keeps you on track, gives you hope and makes you stronger.

_____
_____
_____
_____
_____
_____
_____
_____

70

Section 2
Other Forms
of Composition

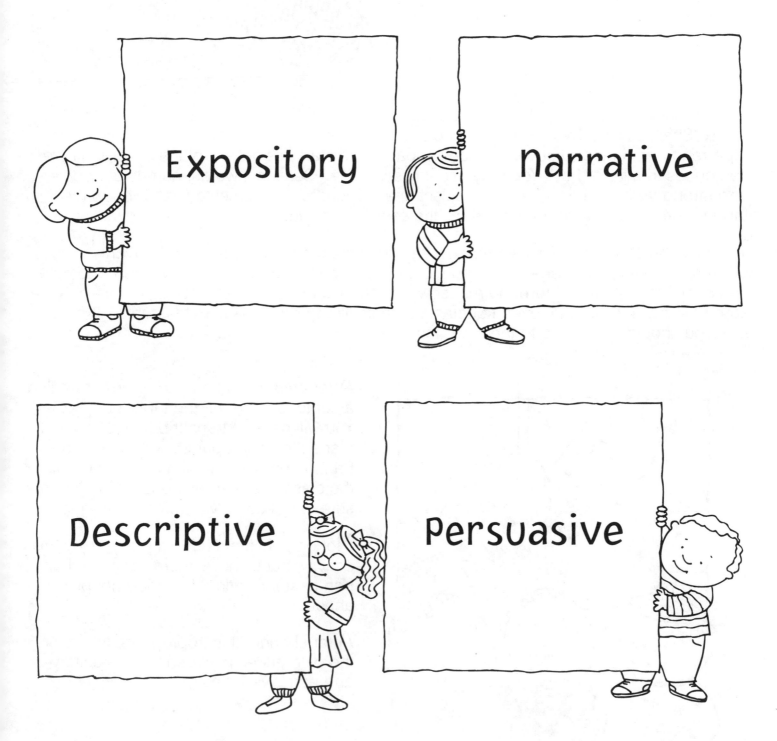

Expository

Narrative

Descriptive

Persuasive

The Narrative Style
Introducing a Different Form of Writing

To introduce this new and very different style of writing you should prepare some kind of an icebreaker activity. Expository writing derives its strength from order, predictability and structure. While these criteria are important in narrative writing, the main purpose of this form is to ENTERTAIN the reader.

An activity that works well to break the ice is the "Shared Narrative." You will need a tape recorder, a jar and several pieces of paper. To start this activity place several different sentences in a jar or hat. You may use any sentence. Seasonal words, names of people and strong verbs are good topics. Select one student to draw a sentence. Turn on the tape recorder. The student then reads the sentence aloud.

Then tell the students, "This sentence is the first sentence of an action and adventure once-upon-a-time story. You are to continue telling that story. The objective is to keep adding a sentence when it is your turn, no matter what comes into your mind." Though there may be some moans and groans, even reluctant students like to participate in this game. If possible, you should contribute to the story, too.

After each child has had a turn at adding a sentence, turn off the tape recorder. You will need to transcribe the story and place it on chart paper or an overhead transparency. Then share the story with the class in a read-aloud fashion. You are sure to get some very creative writing!

Not only do the students really enjoy this activity, but it shows them what can happen to story writing if they do not plan ahead.

After sharing, it is appropriate to explain the differences between the expository and narrative forms.

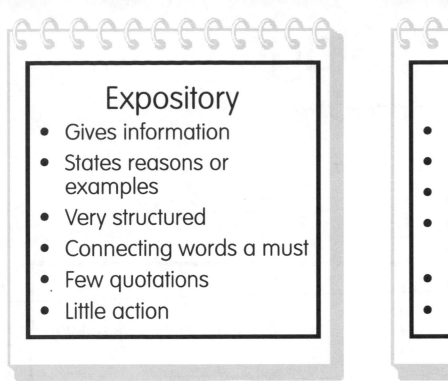

Expository

- Gives information
- States reasons or examples
- Very structured
- Connecting words a must
- Few quotations
- Little action

Narrative

- Entertains
- Has events
- More loosely structured
- Connecting words only as needed for chronology
- More dialogue
- Lots of action

The differences between the two forms can best be exemplified by preparing two basic four squares on a similar prompt. One has reasons, explanations or examples (usually nouns) for boxes 2, 3 and 4; the other has events for these boxes (usually verbs). Which one is telling the entertaining story?

The narrative four square is the one that shows the ACTION.

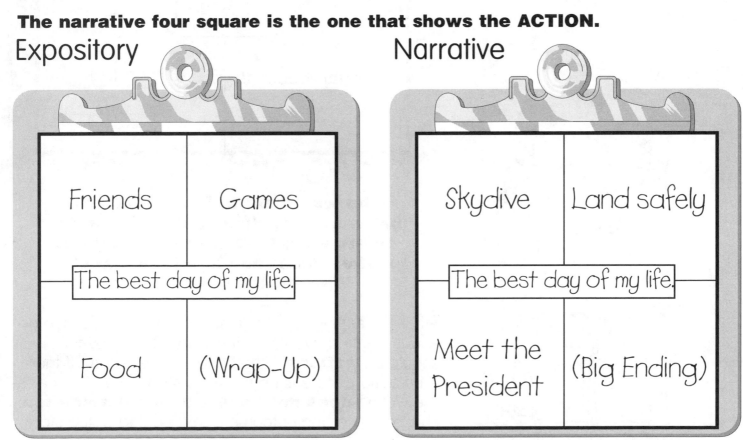

Expository

Friends	Games
The best day of my life.	
Food	(Wrap-Up)

Narrative

Skydive	Land safely
The best day of my life.	
Meet the President	(Big Ending)

The best day of my life will have friends, games and food.

On the best day of my life I will skydive, land safely and meet the President.

4□ Stage
narrative

In the first step of building a narrative four square, students are required to answer the questions Who? What? Where? When? and Why? These questions are aiming at a description of the setting before the problem or action takes place.

The 4□ in a narrative style

Event (think action!)	Event (think action!)
Topic Plus Who? What? Where? When? Why?	
Event (think action!)	Big Ending

Who was there *before the action*?
What were they doing *before the action*?
Where were they *before the action*?
When does the story take place?
Why are the people there?

After the setting is established, the writer needs to go about creating events for the story. These events should be **actions** with strong, active verbs. If there is no action, there is no narrative story! Box 5 in narrative writing **does not have a wrap-up sentence**. This box is for the outcome or big ending of the story.

Name _____

Directions: Complete the setting, three events and an ending for the narrative style four squares.

Event 1	Event 2
_____	_____

A time I disobeyed

Who? _____
What? _____
Where? _____
When? _____
Why? _____
(Before the Action!)

Event 3	Big Ending
_____	_____
	_____
	_____
	_____

Event 1	Event 2
_____	_____

The worst day of my life

Who? _____
What? _____
Where? _____
When? _____
Why? _____
(Before the Action!)

Event 3	Big Ending
_____	_____
	_____
	_____
	_____

Name _____

Directions: Complete the setting, three events and an ending for the narrative style four squares.

Event 1
_____

Event 2
_____

My sibling read my diary

Who? _____
What? _____
Where? _____
When? _____
Why? _____
(Before the Action!)

Event 3
_____

Big Ending
_____

_____

_____

_____

Event 1
_____

Event 2
_____

A really great field trip

Who? _____
What? _____
Where? _____
When? _____
Why? _____
(Before the Action!)

Event 3
_____

Big Ending
_____

_____

_____

_____

4☐ + 3 Stage

narrative

The "+3" step in building a narrative four square is quite similar to the expository form. The details provided will help to elaborate on the events in boxes 2, 3 and 4. In the narrative style, the details can be thought of as a vehicle to explain "how it happened."

The 4☐ + 3 stage in a narrative style

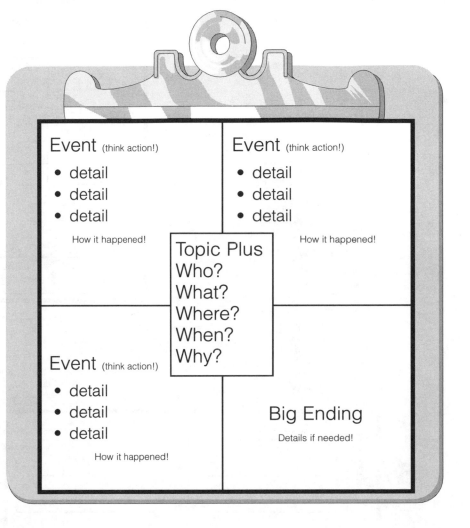

Event (think action!)
- detail
- detail
- detail

How it happened!

Event (think action!)
- detail
- detail
- detail

How it happened!

Topic Plus
Who?
What?
Where?
When?
Why?

Event (think action!)
- detail
- detail
- detail

How it happened!

Big Ending
Details if needed!

It may be useful to compare the details to a description of a scene on television. If a friend had not watched the show, describe everything that you could see.

Remind students to make themselves aware that each box signifies a new event, and they should not get ahead of themselves. Sometimes kids have the tendency to kill off the main characters in a bloody scene even before the action has truly started.

Name _____

Directions: Complete the setting, three events and an ending for the narrative style four squares.

Event 1: _____   Event 2: _____

- _____   - _____

- _____   - _____

- _____   - _____

When I met King Kong
Who? _____
What? _____
Where? _____
When? _____
Why? _____
(Before the Action!)

Event 3: _____   Big Ending

- _____

- _____

- _____

Event 1: _____   Event 2: _____

- _____   - _____

- _____   - _____

- _____   - _____

The field trip that went bad
Who? _____
What? _____
Where? _____
When? _____
Why? _____
(Before the Action!)

Event 3: _____   Big Ending

- _____

- _____

- _____

78

Name _____

Directions: Complete the setting, three events and an ending for the narrative style four squares.

Event 1: _____

• _____

• _____

• _____

_____

How I became President

Who? _____

What? _____

Where? _____

When? _____

Why? _____

(Before the Action!)

Event 2: _____

• _____

• _____

• _____

_____

Event 3: _____

• _____

• _____

• _____

Big Ending

_____

_____

_____

Event 1: _____

• _____

• _____

• _____

_____

My incredible dream

Who? _____

What? _____

Where? _____

When? _____

Why? _____

(Before the Action!)

Event 2: _____

• _____

• _____

• _____

_____

Event 3: _____

• _____

• _____

• _____

Big Ending

_____

_____

_____

4□ + 3 + C Stage
narrative

In the narrative composition, the use of connecting words is at the discretion of the writer. The words used to connect ideas most often in narrative writing are "time connectors." These are employed to show the time relationship between events that occurred. They generally have a dramatic effect. In one story it may be meaningful if something happens IMMEDIATELY. In another story, if something happens 10 YEARS LATER it may be equally shocking.

The 4□ + 3 + C stage in a narrative style

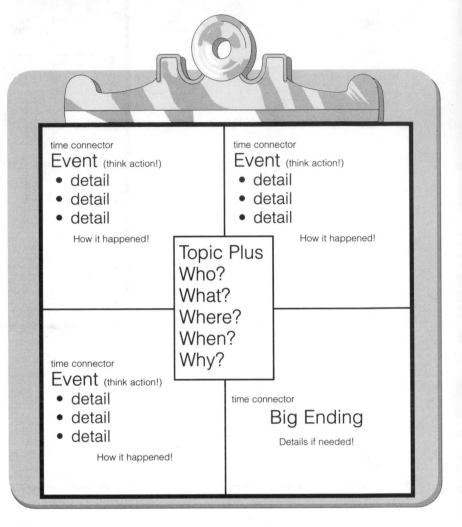

time connector
Event (think action!)
- detail
- detail
- detail

How it happened!

time connector
Event (think action!)
- detail
- detail
- detail

How it happened!

Topic Plus
Who?
What?
Where?
When?
Why?

time connector
Event (think action!)
- detail
- detail
- detail

How it happened!

time connector
Big Ending
Details if needed!

Because of the flexibility of time in creative writing, it is impossible to "spoon feed" these connecting words as was done with expository. If they are troubling for the novice writer, they may be omitted.

An incomplete list of time connectors follows.

Time Connectors

A very incomplete list

First
Next
Then
Last
After that
Immediately
One (second/hour/minute/day/year) later
Soon after that
The next day
Later on
In the beginning
In the end
At (give time)
A long time ago
Long after that
Not long after that
Meanwhile
At the same time
That evening
That morning
That afternoon
Today
Yesterday
Tomorrow
Etc.

"Hooks" to Be Used with Narrative Writing

Several Ways to Engage the Reader from the Start

The function of the narrative style is to entertain the reader. In doing so the writer hopes to attract interest so the reader will want to read the story.

One method of attracting reader interest is the use of a hook. The hook is a one-sentence device placed at the beginning of the story. Hooks are used in an attempt to generate a curiosity in the reader.

The hook is to be followed by the setting and event paragraphs, as usual.

Hooks to Be Used in Narrative Writing

The Question	*Have you ever been afraid to fly? Well I was . . .*
The Quotation	*"Run and don't look back!" my brother shouted.*
Hyperbole	*That pumpkin was as big as a school bus.*
Fragments	*Pennies. Pennies everywhere. Far as I could see.*
Famous Name or Place	*The Statue of Liberty, there she stood.*
Money	*Ten million dollars, and all mine.*

The Descriptive and Persuasive Writing Styles

Going Right or Left of the Expository

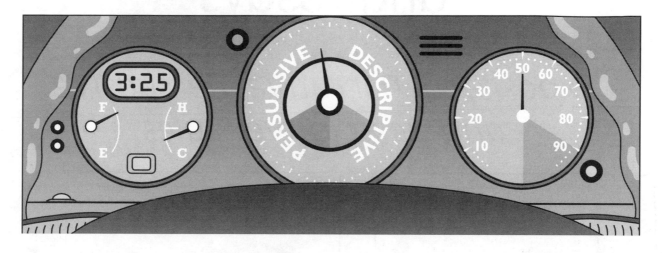

The persuasive and descriptive writing forms are organized in a very similar manner as the expository. The scale above moves from persuasive through expository to descriptive. Because the expository form is a combination of persuasion and descriptive detail, it lies at the midpoint of the scale.

To use four square for the other two styles, a writer will need to be concerned with the difference in the topic sentences for the body paragraphs; the major difference lies in the intent of the information completed in the 4□ + 3 stage.

In the three styles the structure and form are identical. All benefit from the detailed and specific prewriting thought achieved through the use of the four square method.

For examples of four squares and essays in these styles, check the writing examples section.

Section 3
Samples of Four Squares and Essays

Expository, Narrative, Persuasive and Descriptive Styles

Thinking

Planning

Drafting

Revising

Expository

One reason

Big kitchen

- room to cook
- lots of food
- big refrigerator

Also

Fireplace

- warm
- crackling
- smoky smell

My home is a special place.

Third

My porch

- screened
- relaxing
- cool

In summary

My home is a special place because it has a big kitchen, a fireplace and a porch.

Expository Essay

My home is a special place. It is special because it has a fireplace, a big kitchen and a porch. It is a wonderful place to live.

One reason my home is special is because I love my big kitchen. I have plenty of room to cook. There is a lot of room for all the food I like to eat. I like my large refrigerator most of all.

Also, my fireplace is wonderful. On chilly nights it keeps me warm as a mitten. I love to listen to the crackling. The smoky smell reminds me of the days when I go camping.

Third, my home has a terrific porch. The porch is screened, which is lucky for me. I am a bug magnet! My porch is a great place for relaxing. Even on warm nights the porch is cool because you can enjoy the evening breezes.

In summary, my home is special because it has a big kitchen, a fireplace and a porch. I couldn't imagine living anywhere else.

Narrative

In the beginning
   Cat food commercial came on
- dancing cats
- singing about food
- I said "How cute"

During the commercial
      My cat got angry
- arched his back
- his hair stood up
- hissed aloud

The day my pet spoke to me
Who?   My cat and I
What?   Relaxing
Where?   At home
When?   In the evening
Why?   It had been a long day

Just then
      He spoke to me
- called the commercial foolish
- said the food was gross
- told me never to buy it again

Since that day
never spoken again
stopped buying food
My cat is not allowed to watch TV.

Narrative Essay

One evening I was relaxing at home. My cat and I were watching television. It had been a long day, and I needed some time to wind down.

In the beginning of our favorite show, a commercial came on for a brand of cat food I usually buy. This commercial had adorable little dancing cats. The cats were singing about the cat food. I thought it was cute, and I laughed out loud.

During this commercial my cat got angry. He stood up and arched his back. The hair on his back was standing up. He let out an ear-splitting scream.

Just then, he started talking. He called the commercial foolish and snarled at the television. My cat told me that brand of cat food was gross. Then he told me never to buy it again. I had always thought that he liked the stuff!

Since that day my cat has not spoken again. I did stop buying that brand of cat food. But because of his ill-mannered hissing and growling, my cat has had a limit placed on his television time.

Persuasive

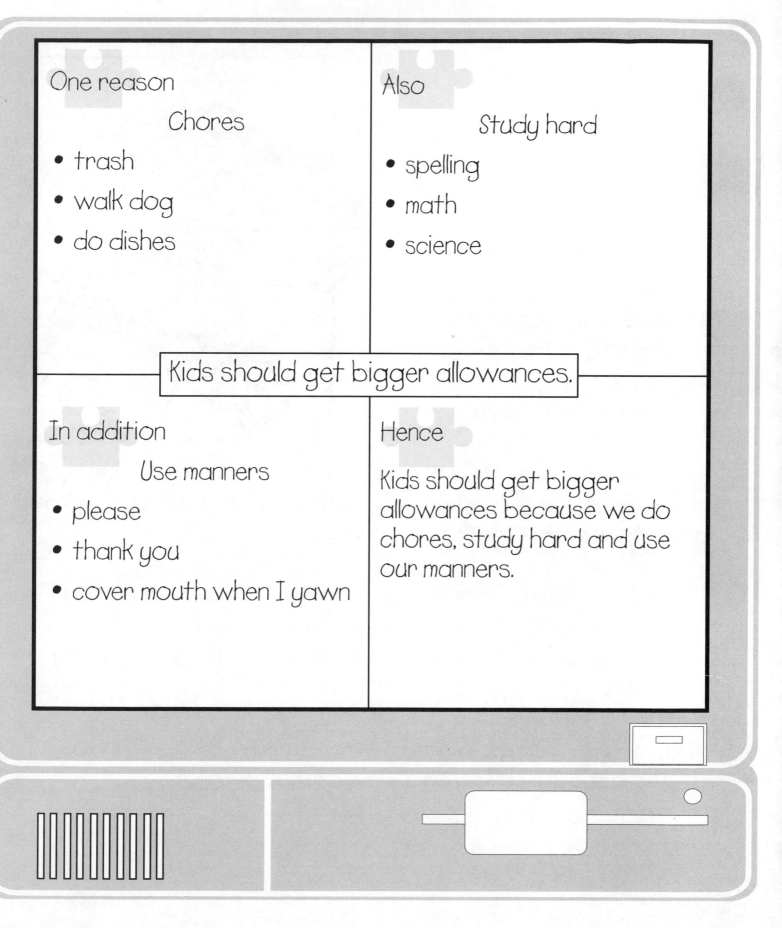

One reason

Chores

- trash
- walk dog
- do dishes

Also

Study hard

- spelling
- math
- science

Kids should get bigger allowances.

In addition

Use manners

- please
- thank you
- cover mouth when I yawn

Hence

Kids should get bigger allowances because we do chores, study hard and use our manners.

Persuasive Essay

Kids should get bigger allowances because we do chores. Kids are always studying hard. We even use manners! It isn't easy being a kid, and we deserve a little reward.

One reason for a larger allowance is all the chores we do. We take out stinky trash every night. Walking the dog is really not fun. And who likes doing dishes?

Also, kids study hard, and that should be worth something. Spelling words take a long time to learn. For math we have to add and subtract. Science homework keeps us busy, too.

In addition, kids use their manners, so they should get something in return. Why do you think we say "please"? "Thank you" is another way we are polite. Let's face it, we don't cover our mouths while yawning for nothing.

Hence, kids should get bigger allowances because we do chores, study hard and use our manners. How can you disagree?

Descriptive

One reason

The grass

- green
- neat
- no weeds

Also

Memorial Park

- plaques
- jerseys
- baseballs

Yankee Stadium is a beautiful place.

Too

The electricity

- always there
- shouting fans
- memory of greatness

As one can see

Yankee Stadium is a beautiful place because of the grass, Memorial Park and the electricity in the air.

Descriptive Essay

Yankee Stadium is a beautiful place. The beauty can be seen in the grass and Memorial Park, and it can be felt in the electricity in the air. I love to visit there.

One reason it is so beautiful is the grass. It is always frog-green. The lawn is manicured and perfectly cut. Weeds are prohibited from entering.

Also, Memorial Park is a special place. One can view the plaques that have been so delicately engraved in remembrance. There are jerseys to view that were well-worn by the greats. They have tattered, old baseballs which have priceless signatures.

The electricity in the air is beautiful, too. It is always there, and you can see it in the eyes of the children visiting. The shouting of the fans sounds like the Mormon Tabernacle Choir to the ears of a baseball lover. One can sense the memory of greatness because their spirits live in the air at Yankee Stadium.

As one can see, Yankee Stadium is a beautiful place because of the grass, Memorial Park and the electricity in the air. You should catch a game today.

Section 4
Four Square and Beyond

Across the Curriculum

Science

Social Studies

Math

The Arts

4□ in the Language Arts Program

Using Four Square as a Part of the Writing Process

Four square helps students organize their thoughts and plans before they write. This makes for better writing. However, four square alone is not a writing program.

Brainstorming

Students need a variety of activities and approaches to spark their interest. A semantic map or sensory web can be used to begin the writing process, and they can help develop the material before organizing with the four square. Students may have a shared experience to develop their writing. Certainly the use of four square does not call for an abandonment of hands-on learning in the language arts.

Organizing

The four square is an elaborate prewriting organizational tool. Four square helps align the writers' thoughts and prepare them for drafting the composition. Because the four square develops the material that will be required in the drafting stage of writing, it helps to eliminate common errors that create a need for rewriting. This is what makes four square the ideal tool for preparing the "write on demand" draft test that many states have adopted as assessments.

Drafting

In this step the student creates a manuscript that is usually full of errors that need correcting, things that need changing and sometimes "scrapping" and starting over. It is a natural step of the writing process, certainly not the last. Because this is the step at which most states take assessment, we need to make the most of the organization. It can help eliminate errors.

Revising and Editing

The structural changes and syntactical errors that appeared in the draft are corrected in this step. A proofreading wall poster follows for duplication (page 97).

94

During the editing of their writing, students should be encouraged to consider their word choices and sentence structure. It is desirable to eliminate "weak" language and get the most bang for your buck. There are two common word choice problems that occur in the primary grades, repeated phrases and weak or ambiguous adjectives.

The repeated phrases are easy to pick out in writing.

My school is great. **You can** go on the playground. **You can** go to music class. **You can** have a lot of fun.

This writer has the "you-can fever," and nearly every emergent writer develops a form of this fever. Once students are aware of it, they are usually eager to correct it. Simply starting the sentence with something other than the subject can eliminate the problem. Also, use of a question (*"Doesn't it sound like fun?"*) can break the fever.

The use of weak adjectives is not as easy for the students to pick out.

My school is great. It is really **cool**. I think *my* school is **awesome**. My school is really **the best**.

What, it any, difference is there between these three sentences? In the student's mind there may be a difference between these three descriptions, but a reader likely won't catch them. To help alleviate this problem, certain words are "illegal" in writing. You can develop this list as need occurs.

Another way to enhance word choice is to encourage stronger adverb and verb selection. To develop this sense, a game of sorts can be played. A sentence with a linking or "weak" verb is given, and students are challenged to write as many strong versions of the sentence as possible.

Last year I went to Miami.
Last year I drove to Miami.
Last year I swam to Miami.
Last year I roller bladed to Miami.
Last year I hopped to Miami.
Etc.

This is a fun exercise, and students can get carried away with it. It also works well with linking verbs.

I am here today.
I stand here today.
I dance here today.
I *juggle* here today.
I back flip here today.
I hokey-pokey here today.
Etc.

Publishing

Occasionally students prepare a composition free of errors and written for others to see. Sharing of published work through anthologies or author's chairs is wonderful for student self-esteem.

Four square is only one step in this process, but it is a critical one and one often not taught. Given only the sensory web or semantic map for brainstorming, a student will not have a clear direction for composition. Four square goes beyond the semantic map and provides a **road map.**

During instruction it is imperative that you model good writing practice daily. Students will learn by your example. Also, create an "author's chair" and use it at least weekly. Writing for a real audience helps students' motivation and style.

96

Punctuation!

Punctuation

Do all sentences end with marks?
Is there a reason for each mark I used?
Did I use at least one question or exclamation?
Do I have commas in my wrap-up sentence?

Organization

Did I follow my four square?
Do I have good details and describing words?
Is it neat and organized looking?

Paragraphing

Do I have at least five paragraphs?
Do I have an introduction and a conclusion?
Do I start my sentences differently?
Are my sentences all complete?

Spelling

Did I sound out problem words?
Did I check a dictionary?
Have I entered the words in my spelling
    dictionary?

Illegal Words

_____

_____

_____

_____

_____

_____

_____

_____

_____

_____

_____

_____

_____

_____

_____

_____

Practical Matters

Tips on Making the Writing Program Work

Supplies

To keep students on task and writing, it is important to have the appropriate hardware readily available. A truckload of pencils and paper is appropriate. It may be cost-effective to use a low-grade newsprint for four square preparation and save lined manuscript paper for drafting and rewriting. These supplies should be accessible to students so that they can restock without interrupting instruction.

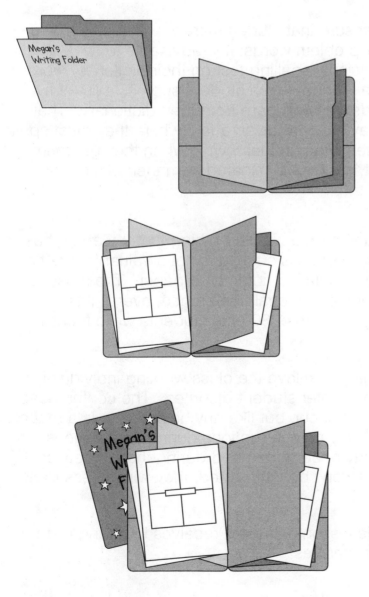

To keep their papers organized, the maintenance of a writing folder is recommended. This folder should have three sections with pockets. The first section in the folder can be used to contain brainstorming activities. The center would hold organizing activities, and the third section would contain compositions. In order to track their work, students should keep a "routing sheet" on the flap of their folders. Each composition has a number, and this number is placed in the upper right-hand corner of every paper generated by the project. The folders should be maintained in a special location in the classroom so that they are not lost or destroyed.

You will also need several overhead transparencies with the four square reproduced on them. Using these with wet-erase markers works quite well for group activities because their work can be shared easily.

Spelling

Spelling is not emphasized throughout four square instruction nor through the writing process. Correct spelling and usage become critical in the publishing stage of the process. Because this is when the work is prepared for a reading audience, the conventional spellings must be used.

Spelling is also an issue when there is a student who refuses to write because he or she cannot spell the words. This is likely to be a student who is not motivated to check a dictionary or reference. In these instances you can provide a conventional spelling under one condition. They must put the spelling in their personal spelling dictionary (a spiral-bound notebook works well). As the year progresses, each student will have more of the common words in their spelling dictionary, and they will ask less often.

To ensure that students are working at learning their problem words, it is advisable to have an occasional spelling test on their dictionary words. On a Monday each student submits a list of five words they will learn from their dictionary. That Friday they are given a test where they must spell those words on their own. When they get them right, they are eliminated from their dictionary!

Conferencing

Practical experience has uncovered that students read almost nothing that a teacher has written on a paper, beyond the grade they achieved. As such, it is not a valuable practice to spend hours grading and writing specific and detailed notes on a paper. The most effective way to aid in student writing growth is the personal conference, even if it is the least time efficient. The trick is how to manage a room of 30-plus students while focusing your attention on one student.

The first requirement is that the others be engaged. Have the class working individually, drafting a composition. This way there will be no inter-student disputes. The conferences can then be called individually. Interruptions will occur, but like anything else, it is a matter of procedure. It is useful to employ an "absolutely no interruptions during conferences" policy. A sign with the message "Not Now" may need to be used during the first few conference sessions. Once students see that you won't be interrupted, they will be less likely to try.

The individual conference is the most valuable lesson a student receives in writing instruction, so don't give up because of management hassles!

100

Other Uses of 4□
in the Language Arts Program

Book Review

The four square form is an excellent method of preparing the book review paper, starting in even the earliest grades. Using this format is less intimidating when they see it in so many different applications.

Speeches

Four square, once mastered, is a fabulous method of preparing notes for speeches or debates. It can contain an entire thesis on one page, including some of the specific details and vivid language intended for use. Once trained in writing from the four square, speaking from it will be an easy task.

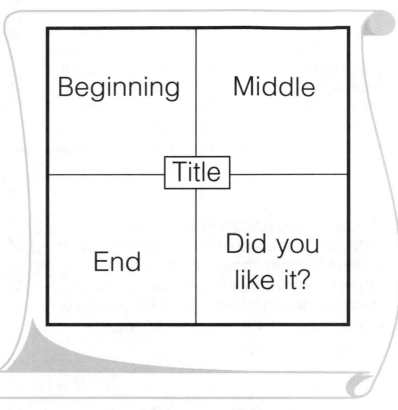

Beginning	Middle
Title	
End	Did you like it?

The four square book review

The 4 □ for Reading Comprehension

Four square can also teach reading comprehension by reading a passage and then building the four square that the writer may have used. One effective way to do this uses the students' own writing. An essay that is well-organized and well-written is prepared on a word processor and printed on heavy-duty paper one sentence at a time. These sentences are then cut up and placed into a can. Each student then draws a sentence until none are left. The objective then is to reconstruct the story. Students must try to find others with similar topics and details. This is a fun and enriching activity. After the story is re-created and read aloud, the original story can be put up on chart paper or overhead transparency. The class then tries to re-create the writer's four square.

4☐ in the Sciences

Using Four Square as a Study Aid

The four square in the expository form adapts well for the sciences. It serves as an excellent way to review or summarize information learned about a specific topic. Using this method to review can provide the student with all the information that is needed for the essay examination, a more authentic form of assessment.

Certainly the occasion will arise when more than three points are made about a topic. Another "box" can be created for other categories of discourse. Once students understand how each box is developed, they will be able to add another box in abstraction.

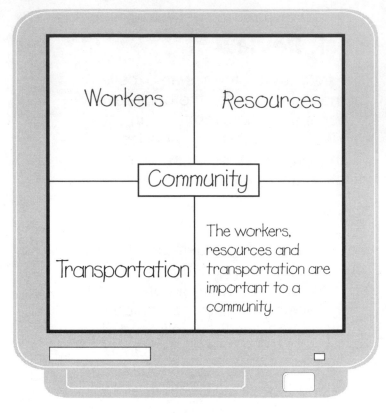

Workers	Resources
	Community
Transportation	The workers, resources and transportation are important to a community.

a four square used in social studies

What are they?	Where are they?
	Volcanoes
How do they operate?	Volcanoes are a powerful, natural force.

a four square used in Earth science

4☐ in Mathematics

Using Four Square to Organize and Solve Word Problems

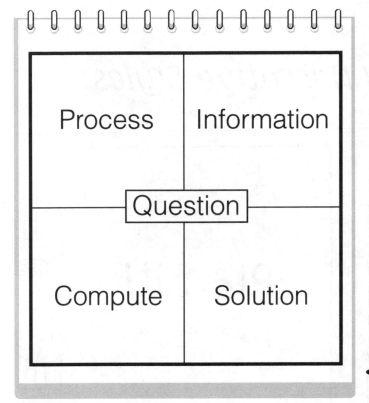

Process	Information
Compute	Solution

Question

W ord problems require the employment of logic and reasoning different from the usual compute-and-solve drills. These problems require that students develop their own equation, and then perform an unnamed operation to find a solution. These steps are not easily completed by the student mathematician.

a four square using the P.I.C.S. formula for word problems

The mathematics formula works using a P.I.C.S. formula. In the "Process" square the student jots down key words. Certainly lessons will be spent decoding the process for particular question key words. The "Information" box is for the collection of numerical data. In the "Compute" box the problem is written and computed. The "Solution" box is the area where the student places the answer, along with any proper terminology.

+	4, 2
1	
4 + 2 = ___	6 "A" Students

1. *Mrs. Rector had four straight "a" students. Then two more students in her class got straight "as." How many "a" students does she have in all?*

Section 5
Practice Prompts

Expository and Narrative Styles

Think It!

Plan It!

Write It!

Do It!

Directions: *Complete the four square plus three plus C. Be sure to include good, vivid language.*

My favorite meal is _____.

Name _____

Directions: Write your five paragraphs based on the four square you just made. Be sure to include good, vivid language in your writing.

Paragraph 1

_____

_____

_____

_____

_____

Paragraph 2

_____

_____

_____

_____

Paragraph 3

_____

_____

_____

_____

Paragraph 4

_____

_____

_____

_____

_____

Paragraph 5

_____

_____

_____

_____

_____

Name _____

Directions: Decide on your setting; then think of three actions and an ending. Add in details to explain the actions. Be sure to include good, vivid language.

_____   _____

_____   _____

_____   _____

_____   _____

_____   _____

When I met Bigfoot

Who? _____

What? _____

Where? _____

When? _____

Why? _____

_____   _____

_____   _____

_____   _____

_____   _____

Name _____

Directions: Write your five paragraphs based on the four square you just made. Be sure to include good, vivid language and lots of action in your writing.

Paragraph 1

_____

_____

_____

_____

Paragraph 2

_____

_____

_____

_____

Paragraph 3

_____

_____

_____

_____

Paragraph 4

_____

_____

_____

_____

_____

Paragraph 5

_____

_____

_____

_____

_____

Directions: Brainstorm three reasons why the place is your favorite. Then write a wrap-up sentence. Give three details for each reason. Add your connecting words. Be sure to use good, vivid language.

My favorite place in the world

Directions: Complete the four square plus three plus C. Be sure to include good, vivid language and factual persuasion.

My school is the best school on Earth.

112